Watch for Hurricanes!

by Rosemarie B. Ferrara

Editorial Offices: Glenview, Illinois • Parsippany, New Jersey • New York, New York
Sales Offices: Needham, Massachusetts • Duluth, Georgia • Glenview, Illinois
Coppell, Texas • Sacramento, California • Mesa, Arizona

Waves caused by hurricane Jeanne hitting the Florida coast in 2004

Did you know that the summer of 2004 was a very busy year for weather reporters on the East Coast of the United States?

It was the summer that thirteen hurricanes formed on the Atlantic Coast. Normally, about five hurricanes develop there during a three-year period, and generally only two become major storms.

What is a hurricane? How can such a storm hurt people? What can people do to protect themselves? Let's find out.

A hurricane is a very strong rain storm. It contains thunder and lightning. It also contains very heavy rain and strong winds.

A rain storm becomes a hurricane when it has winds that blow faster than 74 miles per hour. Hurricane winds can blow faster than 155 miles per hour. Hurricane winds usually blow in a circular direction.

Can you see the circular motion of the wind in this photo? This view is from a satellite in the sky.

---

circular: moving in a circle

This is what a hurricane looks like as it develops.

Saffir-Simpson Hurricane Scale

Category	Definition
One	Winds 74–95 mph
Two	Winds 96–110 mph
Three	Winds 111–130 mph
Four	Winds 131–155 mph
Five	Winds greater than 155 mph

Hurricane winds blow at high speeds, measured in miles per hour (mph).

   In 1969, Herbert Saffir and Dr. Bob Simpson developed a way to measure the strength of a hurricane. They learned that the force of the storm could be measured by how fast its winds blow. They created a special scale to help meteorologists (weather scientists) make accurate weather reports. The Saffir-Simpson Scale, shown above, gives each hurricane a category number based on its wind speed.
   The stronger the hurricane is, the more damage it can cause. It's important for us to know how strong a storm is expected to be so we can take the right precautions.

---

precautions: things done to prevent harm or danger

Bonnie was one of the worst hurricanes to hit the U.S.A. in 1998.

Did you know that each hurricane is given a person's name? Did you ever wonder how the names are chosen?

In 1951 the United States adopted a plan to name hurricanes according to the letters of the alphabet. Hurricanes usually develop on the Atlantic Coast between June 1 and November 30 every year. This is called the *hurricane season*. The first hurricane to form each season is given a person's name beginning with an *A*. The second storm's name begins with a *B*. This pattern continues going down the alphabet until the season ends and no more storms develop.

    Where do the names come from? Hurricane names are chosen years in advance by an international committee called the World Meteorological Organization. The names are placed on a list for each year.

    As soon as an Atlantic tropical storm develops winds that are greater than 74 miles per hour, an agency within the National Weather Service gives the storm a name from that year's list. The number of storms that develop during the year will determine how many names from the list will be used.

Names for Atlantic Tropical Storms

2007	2008	2009
Andrea	Arthur	Ana
Barry	Bertha	Bill
Chantal	Cristobal	Claudette
Dean	Dolly	Danny
Erin	Edouard	Erika
Felix	Fay	Fred
Gabrielle	Gustav	Grace
Humberto	Hanna	Henri
Ingrid	Ike	Ida
Jerry	Josephine	Joaquin
Karen	Kyle	Kate
Lorenzo	Laura	Larry
Melissa	Marco	Mindy
Noel	Nana	Nicholas
Olga	Omar	Odette
Pablo	Paloma	Peter
Rebekah	Rene	Rose
Sebastien	Sally	Sam
Tanya	Teddy	Teresa
Van	Vicky	Victor
Wendy	Wilfred	Wanda

The table above shows the names to be used in the years 2007–2009.

Is your name on any of the lists? Do you know anyone whose name was chosen as a future hurricane name?

This is what an apartment community looked like before and after a hurricane.

Why are people so afraid of hurricanes? What makes hurricanes so dangerous?

Hurricanes are storms that include high speed winds, heavy rains, and storm surges. Storm surges can cause major flooding. The strong winds can also cause tornadoes. Hurricanes can destroy buildings, trees, power lines, and entire cities and coastlines. They can injure or kill people and animals.

---

storm surges: upward waves of water caused by winds
tornadoes: violent storms of whirling wind

Today, meteorologists can give us very accurate weather forecasts. They can also predict a storm's path. That information tells people where the storm is expected.

As a result of knowing when and where a storm will occur, people can do a lot of things to protect themselves and stay safe.

Extend Language **The Suffix *-ous***

The suffix *-ous* can mean "full of." For example, *dangerous* means "full of danger." Can you tell the meaning of the following words?

humorous   joyous   glamorous

What can people do to make themselves and their homes safe? What can you and your family do?

How to Stay Safe During a Storm

— Listen to the radio or TV for up-to-date information.

— Bring all your pets and toys inside.

— Stay indoors unless you are told to evacuate.

— Know where to go if you must evacuate.

— Board up all windows and glass doors.

— Don't drink tap water.

— Watch for fallen electrical wires.

---

evacuate: leave your home to avoid danger

board up: cover up with boards or sheets of wood

tap water: water from the faucet

One of the most helpful things that you and your family can do before a storm to protect yourselves is to prepare a storm safety kit. What would you put inside this kind of supply kit?

Here are some good things to include:

- ✓ bottled water
- ✓ a first aid kit
- ✓ important medicines
- ✓ a portable radio
- ✓ one or two flashlights
- ✓ extra batteries
- ✓ blankets
- ✓ protective clothing and shoes

Can you think of anything else to add?

This is some of the destruction caused by a hurricane.

As you can see, hurricanes can be very dangerous. They can cause a great deal of damage to people, animals, cities, and even beaches. It's important to listen to weather reports once a hurricane is expected in your area. No one can stop a hurricane. No one can change its natural path, but the more you know about the storm, the safer you and your family will be.